LIAM RATCHICK

THE CLICK TECHNIQUE

The Ultimate Guide to Clickback, Learn All the Important Information and Useful Advice On How to Make Money From the Biggest Affiliate Marketplace

Descrierea CIP a Bibliotecii Naţionale a României
LIAM RATCHICK
   THE CLICK TECHNIQUE. The Ultimate Guide to
Clickback, Learn All the Important Information and Useful
Advice On How to Make Money From the Biggest Affiliate
Marketplace / Liam Ratchick – Bucharest: Editura My Ebook, 2020
   ISBN

LIAM RATCHICK

THE CLICK TECHNIQUE

The Ultimate Guide to Clickback, Learn All the Important Information and Useful Advice On How to Make Money From the Biggest Affiliate Marketplace

My Ebook Publishing House
Bucharest, 2020

TABLE OF CONTENTS

FOREWORD

Established in the late 90's, Clickbank's internet market for digital info products helps individuals and businesses draw in the customers they can't find anyplace else online, and supplies affiliate marketers with protected ways to be successful and fruitful in their business attempts.

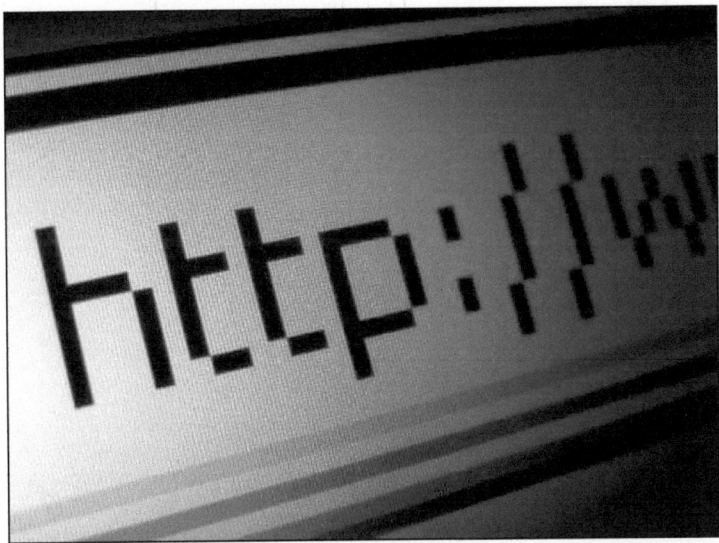

CHAPTER 1

WHAT IS CLICKBANK?

Synopsis

To put it very simply, Clickbank is a virtual marketplace that was founded in 1998. It is a privately held company having offices in Broomfield, Colorado and Boise, Idaho.

Clickbank is an online retail outlet that sells over 50,000 different products.

What Is Clickbank?

What Is Clickbank?

Clickbank is an online retail outlet and an online payment processor. The products featured on Clickbank are digital products like e-books, software, and videos. It is regarded as the best place for people to buy or sell their digital products.

If a person has a digital product or service that they are interested in selling, they can register at Clickbank as a publisher. As a publisher, people can make use of the over 100,000 Clickbank affiliates to find buyers for their products and multiply profits.

Individuals who would like to use the online retailer as a resource to create income can do so as an affiliate. Clickbank affiliates are simply people who market or promote products by publishers and earn commissions.

Every publisher, whenever they publish a product, offers a certain percentage of their product's value as commission to affiliates. Affiliates can earn commissions up to 75 percent.

The payment technology that Clickbank uses allows any publisher or vendor or seller to automatically pay commissions on sales to any affiliate that successfully links a paying customer to that seller. The customer is billed by Clickbank, then the seller is paid and then the affiliate. Clickbank maintains security and quality control over each and every transaction.

Advantages of Clickbank for Vendors/Sellers/Publishers

Clickbank offers many advantages for e-commerce businesspeople. The following are some of those advantages.

Credit Card Payment Acceptance Without Merchant Account

If you are selling an e-book or software and do not have a merchant account, Clickbank allows you to sell your product and accept credit card payments without having to get yourself a merchant account. You can even accept e-checks or online checks. Although Clickbank does require a fee, the ease of being able to accept credit card payments is definitely worth it.

Affiliate Program for Your Product

If you are a vendor, you can create your own affiliate program. You have the freedom to decide the commission percentage that you would like to offer any affiliate who successfully sells your product. You can choose anywhere from 1% to 75% depending on how you would like to structure your affiliate program.

Your Product Is Advertised for Free

As a seller or publisher, your product gets exposure through the free listings on the Clickbank site. Your product will also appear through the search facilities of other sites associated with Clickbank. This means that your product is advertised for free.

Referral Commissions

You can also earn money via referral commissions on the thousands of products in the Marketplace.

Advantages of Clickbank for Affiliates

There are many advantages of being a Clickbank affiliate and some of them are:

No Registration Fee

There are so many different affiliate programs available on the internet. Most of them advertise that joining is free but they charge when someone would like to become an affiliate. Clickbank is free. There are no registration fees and no hidden charges to becoming an affiliate.

Prompt Payment

Unlike most of the other affiliate programs on the net, Clickbank pays regularly and promptly. The payment is given every two weeks and the payments are on time.

Great Products

The sheer number of products available makes it easy for an affiliate to choose the products that he or she would like to promote. Products range from e-books, videos, software and many more. The moment a product that is being promoted by an affiliate sells, a commission is earned.

Great Commissions

The percentages are very good. An affiliate can earn as much as 75% of the value of the sale of a product. This makes Clickbank a lucrative endeavor for many affiliates.

Clickbank Terminologies

There are many terminologies that are unique to each organization or program and the same holds true for Clickbank. If you are new to the online retailer, you may get confused with all the terminologies that may be new to you or different from the site you used to do business with. Here are some of the more common terminologies that you will find as you start your partnership with Clickbank.

Publishers/Vendors

Vendors or Publishers refer to the people who have digital products that they are selling or wish to sell. A person can be both a vendor or publisher and a promoter. The main thing to remember is that a publisher is the one that creates the products being sold.

Recurring Billing

Both promoters (affiliates) and publishers (vendors) will get to meet these two words rather often. Recurring billing refers to subscriptions that pay monthly. If you are offering a product or a membership of some type that requires monthly payments, Clickbank takes care of the nitty-gritty. You only need to relax and wait for the profits.

Promoters

These are the people who promote the products on Clickbank. They are also called affiliate marketers. They go through the Clickbank Marketplace to look for products to promote and find buyers for those products.

Gravity

Gravity refers to which products are not being promoted actively but selling, and which are not doing so well. Simply put, the higher the gravity, the more attractive the product is to affiliate marketers because it means the product sells well.

15

Therefore, if you are a promoter or an affiliate, you need to look for products that have high gravity.

However, this does not mean that you should not sell products with low gravity. There are products that may not be selling well simply because no one has taken the time to promote it properly.

There are many more words and phrases that you will come across as you develop your partnership with Clickbank. It does help if you take the time to learn about what the words and phrases mean as they play a role in your dealings with the online retailer.

CHAPTER 2

WHY CLICKBANK?

Synopsis

What is it about Clickbank that makes it so popular? What makes it a great business opportunity? Why Clickbank?

Why Clickbank?

First and foremost, you will need to understand what Clickbank is. Clickbank is an online retailer. It is the largest digital information site today with an affiliate program network. This simply means that it acts as a gateway for publishers and affiliates. This is what makes it relatively easy for anyone to find products that they can promote and earn hefty commissions from.

One of the biggest pluses about Clickbank is that it is easy to set-up an account with. This makes it easy for you to start earning money right away. It uses a "hoplink" system that allows you to insert your affiliate ID. All you need to do is create a nickname that is embedded in your selected product's URL and you can start selling or promoting the product.

Becoming a Clickbank affiliate is also free. There are no registration fees, no hidden charges and no other fees that will be charged if you decide to become an affiliate. You can simply go to the site, choose to become an affiliate and register. Once you do that, you can go ahead and browse through the products available in the Marketplace and choose those that you want to promote. You then proceed to promoting those products and then earn commissions on every sale that you make. Remember that you can earn anywhere from 10% to as much as 75% of the sale value as commission on any sale that is made through your promotion efforts.

If you have an existing home based business website, or blog, you can start making money with no need of creating a product of your own. This is very important because most promoters have problems regarding creating products that will sell. Clickbank gives you a wide choice of products to promote so you can earn money right away.

Another of the biggest pluses of affiliate marketing is that you get to earn by selling someone else's products. Clickbank is the same, except for the fact that the products in Clickbank are digital products like software, e-books, subscriptions or videos.

With Clickbank you have options regarding how to sell the products. A lot of the affiliate retailers promote products on their Clickbank websites and earn commissions. Others put links on their home based business websites. You have a choice about how you can sell the products. You can choose the option that works best for you.

On the other hand, if you are a vendor or a publisher, Clickbank is a very good place to feature your product because you have the leverage of the hundreds of thousands of affiliate marketers that can promote your product on the web. All you need to do is create a selling page for your product that is well designed and well written so that affiliates will find it attractive and choose to sell your products. This makes it easy for you to start earning for your product that is being promoted and sold by someone else.

Clickbank takes care of the all the payment transactions by customers who buys products. This means that publishers need not go through the trouble of getting a merchant account with credit card companies. Clickbank will accept the payments in e-checks or credit cards. This gives publishers more freedom to work on their next product instead of worrying about transactions.

Clickbank is built on a platform that truly works. People get paid regularly and on time. Products get delivered and it is a win-win for all concerned. For all the ten years that Clickbank has been in business, it prides itself on never being late for payment even once. Considering the sheer numbers of transactions that they handle on a daily basis, their ability to keep track of who gets paid and paying those people on time is not something to be taken lightly.

Clickbank also handles recurring billing subscriptions or memberships through its Marketplace. Anyone with an account can offer up to 500 products. This means that mixing in a few recurring billing products to an affiliate's portfolio or products means a regular monthly income.

Clickbank has been doing business for so many years especially in the service of credit card payment online. Now, they are also accepting PayPal as a way to pay for products sold in Clickbank marketplace. It gives more flexibility to online users.

Another great plus for Clickbank is that it has been in the business for many years and has built up a name and a reputation as being a brand that can be trusted. Customers know that their credit card details are safe. In this day and age where there are many cases of online customers getting defrauded, being secure in the knowledge that your credit card information is safe means everything.

This is also a big advantage for affiliates as they can be confident that the buyers who buy the products they are promoting will not face any problems. Publishers can also rest assured that their products are being sold in a legitimate and responsible site.

Clickbank also handles all the transactions involving payment of commissions to affiliates. This means that publishers can rest easy and focus on developing new products to sell.

Publishers will not have to keep track of who sells what when and how much is due that affiliate. Clickbank takes care of everything.

Clickbank even issues refunds when required. Publishers can go on creating new products without any added stress. All this is available for only a small fraction of the total price of the products. Considering all the advantages, it seems more like a wise investment.

Clickbank also provides its partners with the information that really matters. They provide real-time tracking reports. This means that whenever there is a sale of your product, you can login to your account and see the sales records. You can also check the performance of your promotion efforts at any time night or day.

CHAPTER 3

GETTING STARTED

Synopsis

Clickbank is deemed to be the leading site for selling digital products. There are more than 12,000 publishers or vendors that sell different products on the site and there are about 100,000 affiliate marketers that are registered with the site.

Getting Started

If you are interested in making income while being within the comforts of your own home, Clickbank may be the perfect thing for you. You can earn money either by selling digital products that you have created (like e-books, videos or software), or by becoming an affiliate and promote products that other people have created.

Publisher or Vendor

Getting started on Clickbank is simple. All you need to do is follow these steps and you are well on your way to becoming an internet entrepreneur.

Go to the Clickbank site and register for an account. Registering is free and there are no joining fees.

Take a moment and think about how you would like to earn money. Would you find it better and more suitable to create a product like an e-book and sell it? Or would you rather just promote a product that was made by someone else? The choice is all yours.

If you decide to be a vendor or publisher, you will need to create your product. Make sure that the product you create is unique and creates value for a person who may buy it. The best way to find out if it is any good is to think as a customer, look closely and honestly at your product and ask "what's in it for me if I buy this?" If the pluses (advantages of using the product) outweigh the minuses (expense of buying the product), then you are on the right track.

Once you have your unique and high-quality product, you need to design your sales page. Include a picture or graphic of your product to make the page more exciting and interesting. Write a great sales pitch about what the product can offer people who will buy it. Have testimonials by real people. Make a "thank you" page too.

Complete a form on Clickbank and submit it for approval. Once Clickbank approves your product, log in to your account and pay a small investment of $49.95 as activation charges. Once your payment has been processed, you can begin selling your products.

Make use of the affiliate marketers by writing an email requesting that your product be listed in the Clickbank marketplace. Specify the category you would like to have your product classified as.

Once your product is listed in the marketplace, affiliate marketers can now help promote your product for you so that you can sell more of them and earn good money.

Affiliate Marketer

If you would rather promote a product that has been created by someone else, here are the steps on how you can get started.

Log in to your Clickbank account. Go to the marketplace and browse through the products that are listed there. Choose a product that you feel you would be able to promote effectively. When choosing a product you need to make sure that you opt for one that has a gravity of about 50% or higher. Gravity refers to the potential of the product to sell. The higher the gravity, the higher the potential of that product is. However, this does not mean that products of lower gravity percentages are useless. If you find a product that you believe is of good quality and of value to customers, you can always choose that product and promote it.

Once you have chosen a product, under that product, there is an option that says "create hoplink." Type your account nickname on the field provided and click the "create hoplink" button. Copy and paste the hoplink onto a notepad or any other word processing software and safe onto your pc. This will help you in your efforts to promote the product. Hoplinks are links that take the customer, once they click the link, to the start page of the vendor.

The next step is using your hoplink. You can now use your hoplink and incorporate it into your blog, or website. Or you can promote it by writing articles and submitting them to article directories, using pay-per-click and many more. If you have a website or blog, you can incorporate the hoplink into your pages or blog entries.

Whenever a customer clicks the hoplink that customer is taken to the sales page of the publisher where a sale will, hopefully, be made and you will earn your commission.

Whether you are an affiliate or a publisher, you need to make sure that your product is something unique. Another important thing is to choose a product that is not in a category where there are already hundreds or thousands of other competing products. Creating or promoting something that has to compete with so many other products in the same category may mean you will have a tougher time getting sales.

Also worth noting is that you need to be patient. Do not give up if your attempt at selling does not produce instant results. Instead take time to learn where the problem lies because it will help you improve. Being involved with Clickbank is a business and like any business it needs time to grow and develop.

Keep focusing your efforts on selling your product. Be confident and learn from your experiences. Success does not come overnight. It takes a lot of effort. Look closely at your product. If you are an affiliate and you feel that you have tried your very best but things are not working out, try choosing another product and see if that helps.

If you are a vendor and your product does not sell but you truly believe in it, maybe your start page needs more work. Write a better sales pitch. Include a video testimonial. Upload a more attractive product photo. Offer your affiliates a better deal. Maybe they are not attracted to your product because the commission you offer is not at par with others within the same category.

Clickbank can provide you with countless opportunities to earn money provided you use it effectively and invest time and effort.

CHAPTER 4

SIGNING UP FOR A CLICKBANK ACCOUNT

Synopsis

Clickbank is an online retailer specializing in digital products. It was founded in 1998 and is the marketplace chosen by a vast majority of vendors to sell their products. It also has a very popular affiliate marketing program that has over 100,000 active affiliate marketers.

Signing Up for a Clickbank Account

If you are interested in joining Clickbank, you can do so by choosing one of two options. You can open a Clickbank Affiliate Account which allows you to market and promote digital products of your choosing, or you can open a Clickbank Vendors Account which allows you to sell your digital products.

Clickbank Affiliate Account

Having an affiliate account allows you to choose among the many thousands of digital products in the Clickbank marketplace and promote it. When the product you are promoting gets sold because of your efforts, you earn a commission that can range anywhere from 1% to 75%.

Becoming an affiliate member costs you nothing. There are no registration fees or joining fees involved. To become a Clickbank affiliate you need to have a valid email Id, a permanent address where you can receive your commission checks, a working phone number where you can be reached, and you must be at least 18 years of age.

To sign-up as an affiliate, you need to go through the following steps:

- Go to the Clickbank website and click on the sign-up link.

- Fill-up the online form with the correct information. You need to ensure that you fill in all the fields correctly and with complete information. Any incorrect information may become the cause of getting your payment withheld.

- Choose an account nickname. When choosing a nickname, choose one that you can easily remember. You also need to enter a password. Make sure you choose a password that you will not forget. This is very important as your nickname and password are crucial for you to be able to login.

- You then need to review the Client Contract and check the box that indicates that you have read it and understood it.

- You will be taken to a page that says "sign-up not yet complete" which means that a confirmation code has been sent to your email address which you have used during the sign-up

- Open you email. There will be a link that you will need to click which takes you to a page that requires your 8-digit confirmation code to be entered. Copy-paste the confirmation code from your email to the field in the confirmation page. You will then be requested to enter the captcha code.

You are then successfully registered and you will be taken to the login page.

Clickbank Vendor Account

Having a vendor account allows you to sell a digital product that you have created. There is an initial fee of $49.95 to promote your product(s). The advantage you then have is that there are thousands of affiliates that can promote your product for you and once your product gets sold, you will get paid and this income will keep coming as long as your products are selling.

Whichever account you choose to have, you will be able to take advantage of Clickbank's well-oiled machinery. Clickbank offers a safe payment processing gateway wherein customers can pay using their credit cards so vendor's need not go through the process of getting merchant accounts. Plus, affiliate commissions are computed and paid-out by Clickbank which gives the vendor's less stress and enables them to focus on creating new products. Having a Clickbank account can mean huge earning potential for you whether as a vendor or as an affiliate.

To sign-up as a Clickbank vendor, you need to follow the following steps:

- Go to the Clickbank website and click on the sign-up link on the top of the page

- Fill-up the required fields with the complete and accurate information.

- Choose an account nickname. Make sure that you choose a nickname that you are unlikely to forget. Then choose a password. Remember that you will need these for logging in so choose carefully. Your password must be secure yet easy to remember.

- You then need to read and understand the Client Contract and check the box that indicates that you have read it.

- You will be taken to a page that says "sign-up not yet complete" and you will then need to check your email for the confirmation mail that will be sent by Clickbank.

- Open your email. You will get an email from Clickbank which contains an 8 digit conformation code and a link. Click on the link and you will be taken to a page wherein you will need to enter the 8 digit confirmation code and enter a captcha code.

You are then successfully registered and you will be taken to the login page where you can start using your account.

Whether you want to be an affiliate or a vendor, the sign-up process is the same so you need not worry about having to choose right away what type of account you need to have.

After you have your account, you will need to fill in information on the "My Account" page. All your primary account information, and, your contact and payment information, are all controlled under "My Account."

Make sure that all the information is correct and complete as checks that will be issued to you by Clickbank will be sent to the address that you provide. If there are any errors in the address, you may never receive your checks. Any tax information will be on that page as well so you need to ensure that you enter the correct information.

Having a Clickbank account allows you to take advantage of the opportunities that are open to you as an affiliate, or a vendor. With a small initial investment of time, effort and patience you will be able to generate good income for yourself within the comforts of your own home. You can earn income either by selling digital products that you have created as a vendor, or by promoting products someone else has created as an affiliate marketer.

CHAPTER 5

USING YOUR HOPLINK

Synopsis

If you are a Clickbank affiliate marketer, one of the most important things that you need to learn is how to make use of a Hoplink.

Using Your Hoplink

What Is a Hoplink?

A Hoplink is a URL that is meant to use as referral tracking. It may initially appear just like any ordinary wed address, but these URLs are actually very special. This is because a hoplink routes traffic to Clickbank's referral tracking system. Each and every hoplink includes customized information that takes a person who clicks on the link to the vendor's website which is where they will hopefully buy the vendor's product.

The tracking system is able to identify who was the affiliate marketer that referred the customer. If a customer clicks on a link that contains your hoplink and that customer buys a product within 60 days, then you will be credited with the sale and you will earn your commission.

Hoplinks Creation

There are two ways to create a hoplink if you are an affiliate marketer. The first way is by automatically creating the hoplink using Clickbank's marketplace. You browse through the products and choose which one you would like to promote and then choose the promote button.

You will then be given an automatically generated hoplink that has been specially generated for you. All you need to do now is copy the hoplink URL and paste it where you are promoting the product.

The second way to create a hoplink is by using your Clickbank account nickname and the nickname of the vendor whose products you want to promote. This means you need to know both nicknames to make it work.

Once you have your hoplink, you need to test it to see if it works. You will need to copy-paste the link onto your browser and see if it takes you to the vendor's page. If it does, click the order now button and look at the bottom of the order form, you nickname should appear. Clickbank offers an extra encryption tool that will allow you to make your hoplink address for extra security.

Inserting Hoplink to a Web Page or Blog

Clickbank makes it easy for bloggers and webmasters to make some money by becoming affiliates and promoting any of the many digital products it sells within the marketplace.

If you have your own website or blog, you can take advantage of the opportunity to earn some extra income by becoming an affiliate marketer and using your website or blog to promote the products you have chosen to sell.

You can do that by placing links that are called hoplinks onto your web page or blog so that any customer who clicks on the link can be taken to the vendor's start page which will hopefully entice that person to buy a product and you can earn commission income.

Create an account at Clickbank. Login and browse through the thousands of digital products on the marketplace and choose products that are related to the niche your blog or website belongs to.

This means you should find products that fit well with your website or blog. For example, if you blog about the latest apps for mobile phones then an e-book on how to design apps may be a good fit.

Under the product that you have chosen, there is an option that says "create hoplink." Type your account nickname on the field provided and click the "create hoplink" button. Copy and paste the hoplink onto a notepad or any other word processing software and safe onto your PC.

Go to your blog and log in to the administration panel. Click on the option to create a post and write a new post entry about something that fits perfectly with your product choice. Make sure that you choose a relevant spot to add your hoplink.

Highlight the text that you want to turn into a link and click "insert link" from your blog's panel. Copy the hoplink that you have saved in your pc and paste on the link field. Click the "save" option so that the hoplink gets saved. Then post or publish your blog entry. Your blog now has your hoplink embedded in the chosen word or text.

If you are a webmaster, open the HTML editor and locate the text which you would like to convert into a link.

Copy the HTML code, <a href="URL">Link text</a> into the location of the chosen text or word.

Copy the hoplink that you have saved on your computer and highlight the "URL" in the HTML code.

Replace that with the hoplink. Replace the "link text" with the text that you have chosen to convert into a link and then save the changes.

Inserting Hoplink to an Article

If you have neither a website nor a blog, you can still become an effective Clickbank affiliate marketer by writing articles and submitting them to article directories.

Write an article using any word processing program on your computer. Write articles of at least 400 words as most article directories will not accept articles that are shorter than that.

Ensure that you are writing a quality article about a topic that is related to the product you are promoting.

Create an account or register on any article directory of your choice. Once you have an account, log in and choose the option to write an article.

Copy and paste the article that you have saved onto your computer onto the field provided by the article directory for your article.

Go to the author bio field and write a few lines about yourself or write a short sales pitch about your product. Choose which text to use and convert as a hoplink.

Copy the hoplink that you have saved on your computer and paste onto the chosen text or word.

Submit or publish your article. Your article now contains your hoplink.

Write as many articles as you want and you can submit them to the same directory (just makes sure your articles are original and unique) or submit them to different directories.

CHAPTER 6

PAYMENT RELIABILITY

Synopsis

There are a lot of people who go in for Clickbank affiliate programs. This is because Clickbank commissions are always regular and always on time. Clickbank has the reputation of never being late in sending their checks to the many thousands of affiliate marketers since they first started.

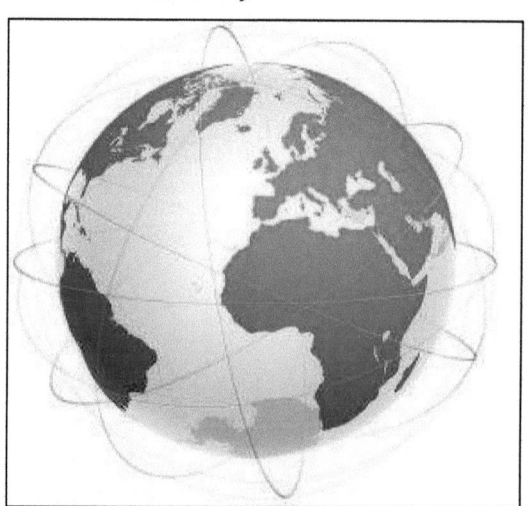

Payment Reliability

Affiliate marketers who are looking for an automated way working from their home can take advantage of the affiliate programs offered by Clickbank. The biggest advantage being that registration as an affiliate is easy and free.

If you are a newbie in affiliate marketing, being able to earn by promoting someone else's products can be confusing at first. With Clickbank, you will need to first register and then find a set of products to promote. Then you need to create a Hoplink after which start promoting the products.

When a customer sees the Hoplink and clicks on it, he or she is taken to the publisher's website. If that customer buys a product, then you get your commission.

The commission you will get depends in the sales price of the product that you have sold and it is then credited to you in your account about two to three minutes after the sale is closed.

It should be worth noting that each and every Clickbank product has a commission rate. The commission rate is set by the product's publisher or vendor and it can be anywhere from

1% to 75% of the selling price of the product. The maximum commission that you may be able to earn per product is $150.

Once a customer buys a product you have promoted, Clickbank takes care of the payment transactions, it then applies any charges on the sale and then your commission is calculated based on the net sale value.

In order for you to receive your first commission earnings, you need to fulfill two requirements. First, you need to reach your payment threshold which you yourself have set in your account settings. Second, you need to meet the requirements as under the Customer Distribution Requirement. If you meet both requirements, you can then start receiving your commission earnings.

After you have received two checks via ordinary mail from Clickbank, you become eligible for receiving a direct crediting of your earnings in your account via direct deposit.

One important thing you need to remember is that when a product is returned by a customer, or if the customer requests a refund, then you will not be able to get your commission. Clickbank returns the money to the customer so the portions of your earnings and the vendor's earnings are returned as well. Clickbank uses a return allowance policy to cover situations involving refunds and returns.

In order to take full advantage of Clickbank's payment reliability, you need to ensure that you promote your chosen products well. It all starts with your choice of products to promote.

After you have created your Clickbank account, you need to browse through the marketplace and look for products that you feel you can promote very well. You need to check the product's gravity. Ideally, you should choose a product whose gravity is 50 or higher so that it has a high selling potential. However, this does not mean that you cannot choose a product that has less gravity if you truly believe that you can sell the product effectively.

After choosing a product, you now need to think about how to promote that product effectively. There are many ways you can do this. If you are a good writer, you can try article marketing. This means that you will write articles about the niche in which your product belongs to and submit it to article directories.

In the part where the directory asks for the author's bio, you can include information about your product and a link which features your affiliate ID. Once a reader of that article clicks on the link, they will be taken to the product vendor's landing page or your own site's landing page.

In order to make sure that you take full advantage of all article writing has to offer, you will need to submit articles to more than one article directory in order to spread out your promotional efforts as wide as possible.

This last step will really be the main part of this article. Once you have an article ready to be published, you will want to get it as much publicity as possible. So in this order, submit to these sites. There are hundreds of article sites online that will accept your articles provided they are high-quality and are not plagiarized copies of other articles that have already been published by someone else.

You can also promote your product via social networking. You can create a page for your product and promote it to your friends and this makes the promotional effort visible to their friends and so on.

There are so many ways you can promote products online and you are free to try them and take full advantage of those methods. Remember that the more exposure a product gets, the higher the chance it will sell and once it sells, you earn a commission on the sales. The more sales you make, the more your earnings will be.

The largest digital marketplace that is Clickbank is an efficient machine that allows you to earn money by simply promoting someone else's product. Although the job of promoting a product may mean you need to put in a lot of effort, it still means that you are selling an already existing product and need not worry about creating your own.

Also, becoming a Clickbank affiliate is affordable because you need not pay anything to become one. Clickbank offers you great earning potential by working from within the comforts of your own home selling an already made product using tools that are provided by the publishers and vendors themselves in most cases.

Clickbank also guarantees that you get the commission income that is due to you regularly and promptly so you can enjoy the fruits of your labors.

CHAPTER 7

PROFITABILITY AS A MERCHANT

Synopsis

The idea behind Clickbank is quite simple. It allows merchants to promote their chosen digital products easily and quickly online.

Clickbank takes care of accepting payments and handling payment transactions, delivering the products, and ensuring that the merchant that sold the product gets the appropriate commission on time.

Profitability as a Merchant

Most of the links that are available in the vast majority of websites these days use Clickbank to handle their sales. This is because Clickbank is very easy to set-up and use. It is secure and is economical for merchants.

Using Clickbank also means that merchants can get the invaluable assistance provided by the many affiliates that promote products. These are people who will actually do the selling of the products to customers.

There are two ways that a merchant can make money by using Clickbank. A merchant can either sell his or her own product, or promote someone else's product. Both of these methods necessitate most of the same skills but being a promoter is easier as you do not have to create a product.

As a merchant on Clickbank, finding success is a matter of getting things right. Once you sign in to the Marketplace, you will see that there are so many products that are being sold by a lot of different people.

The thing is not everyone will be successful. Sales can dip due to a variety of reasons. But if you would like to increase your chances of success, here are some tips to help you become a profitable Clickbank merchant.

The first thing you need to have in order to be profitable is to have a unique product. Many merchants simply go with the flow and create products that are simply copies of other products in the hope that they will do well. You need to create a product that clearly adds value to a customer when he or she buys it.

Something that actually answers a need or provides a solution to a problem or is a new way of presenting something that has been around a long time. Simply making a copycat product of something that is already around may prove to be more of a curse than anything.

One of the most important things that you need to understand as a merchant is that you need to have real life, honest, believable testimonials viewable on your sales page. Sales copy is designed to convince people about what is in it for them if they buy your product.

You need to ensure that testimonials are able to attract your prospective customer's attention enough to convince them to buy. You can do this by using testimonials from real people. Display their full names, their photo and their web address. This makes the testimonial be more authentic than one that says "It's a great product. – from Bob."

Video testimonials would more effective because prospective customers can see real people talking about your product.

Testimonials give sales copy a big boost and this helps sales go up.

Videos do not have to be major cinematic productions as customers may perceive such elaborate videos as "staged" or "made up" just to sell something. Short video testimonials work best.

Another great tip is to have a photo or a graphic of your product available for your affiliates to use when they promote your product. The photo or graphic also need to be on your sales page. Pictures tend to grab more attention and affiliates can use them to attract customers to buy your product. Because online shopping means customers can't physically touch products, they want to be able to get some sort of validation about what it is they are buying. Pictures help them do that.

Another tip is to make sure that the order link is clearly visible and very obvious. People will not spend much time on a sales page when they can't find something that stands out.

Make sure that your order link or order button is clearly noticeable. Make it as big as you possibly can without drowning out your sales page. And have more than one order link or order button spread out all over the page.

However, it is also important to note that your sales page should not contain only order links and order buttons or customers will get put-off.

Your sales copy should be short, simple and written well. People will not read thousands of words. Remember that you have only a few seconds to grab someone's attention. That is what the picture of your product and the first line of your sales page do.

Ensuring that the person's interest is piqued enough to read through the first few lines of your sales pitch depends on how well it is written. A sales page that is full of nothing but text will not be successful. A sales page that has a sales pitch written in language that only someone with a background in particle physics can understand is not going to do well either. Keep things simple, short and interesting. Your affiliates will appreciate it too.

Another thing you need to understand as a merchant is that you need to be patient and not give up. There are hundreds of thousands of digital products out there and it may take time for your product to make its way through the crowd of products. It will take some time before you start seeing any response for your products. And it may take some more time after that to actually have people falling over themselves to buy it.

If your product is unique or provides a solution to a problem, is of high-quality, and is of value to the customer who buys it, you will find buyers. Patience is required.

Clickbank is a great place for merchants to sell their products and if used properly, it can be very profitable. The key is to create a product that is unique, prepare a well- researched and well-studied sales page with attractive photos and realistic testimonials, and have some patience as your product makes its way to customers.

CHAPTER 8

PROFITABILITY AS AN AFFILIATE

Synopsis

Clickbank is a third party affiliate network which means that they are the liaisons between publishers or merchants and the affiliates.

Clickbank makes sure that the merchants' merchandise is promoted and they make sure that their affiliates are paid their commissions on time for every sale that they made.

Profitability as an Affiliate

For merchants, the site is a great forum to sell their digital products and get leverage through over 100,000 affiliates. They know that their products will get the best chances of being sold.

If you are looking for an affiliate program that promises to give you the chance to make good commission earnings, then Clickbank is the best place for you. Getting signed-up is very easy and also free. There are no registration fees or joining fees involved and there are no hidden charges.

In order to be a profitable affiliate, you need to understand that being a Clickbank affiliate is a real business and businesses are built through repeat business. If someone buys a product from you, that person is highly likely to buy from you again. So you need to focus your energies on making your business work.

The key to a stable affiliate commission income is repeat business as it is always easier to sell a product to someone who has already bought something from you.

Choose Your Niche and Your Products

You need to take time to think about your niche. What types of products would you want to sell? Then you should choose a series of products within that niche to market or promote.

If you are interested in gold and feel that you would do well promoting products related to golf then by all means choose that as your niche. If you believe that you can promote lifestyle-related products best, and then go for that.

Choose the Program That Works For You

The next step is to make a plan about how you can promote the products that you have chosen. Choose a method that works for you.

If you are a great writer, you can create an e-book related to the niche you have chosen and offer it for free after making sure that there is a squeeze page or a sales page promoting your Clickbank products.

Or, if you have a website, you can have links to the products you are promoting. There are so many ways you can promote products. Let your imagination take flight. The key is, go with your strengths and choose what you are familiar with.

If you are a blogger, then you can promote your Clickbank products through your blogs. There is also article marketing, social media, pay per click, press releases and many more ways of promoting products that are available.

Capture Leads

Whichever method you choose to promote your products, you need to have a mechanism that captures leads. This means that whether you are giving away an e-book as a means to attract customers or giving links on your website, you need to have a way to get to know about the people who visit your page.

This can be in the form of a place where customers can leave their email addresses. For an e-book giveaway, you can make the download of the e-book in the form of a download link that people will get in their email. Or a direct download link after they give their email.

This will provide you with a list of people who are interested in the niche enough to have given you their email address. They are now your leads. Capture them.

Regular Communication Is Important

Once you have your leads, you can now send regular emails at certain intervals to help you pitch your products. Just ensure that the emails contain quality content and are not spam. A newsletter would be a good idea. This helps you build a relationship with your leads.

Put some links on the email that would help promote your Clickbank products or have some simple squeeze lines to help sell your products.

After Sales Service Is Key

Once a customer has bought a product, never think that your relationship with that person has ended. It has actually just begun. Keep in touch with that customer and make sure you regularly send them a copy of your newsletters or emails. Treat that customer as a lead again.

Remember that a customer who has already bought a product once is likely to buy again. Take care of that customer.

Offer the customer related products to the one he or she has just bought.

Mix in Some Recurring Income Generating Products

Whenever you are building your portfolio of Clickbank products chose a couple of products that can help you earn recurring income. These are products that involve monthly memberships or subscriptions. These are important as they mean a regular monthly income that can truly help you with your affiliate business.

Your success depends on the amount of effort you put in. You need to be focused, consistent, patient and you need to be a quick learner. This is very important because you may face a situation where in your promotional efforts may not be working for you and you need to adapt a new approach. There are many Clickbank vendors or publishers who offer a wealth of marketing and promotional materials. Many even offer sales pages, pictures, video testimonials, articles and blog posts. You can use any materials that they provide you however you see fit.

Clickbank's affiliate program is a very good business option. There are many affiliates who have found earning very good money. The key is to keep in mind that there are no quick fixes. You will need to work and you will need to invest time and effort into your business.

The best part of being an affiliate comes when you get a sale and the commission comes in. But do not rest on your laurels and keep at it. This will help you to keep earning and building a customer base that will be advantageous to you in the long run.

WRAPPING UP

Summing up, Clickbank is an excellent electronic network, with an easy and simple to utilize system, simple sign up process and effective support. Although there are a couple of things that could be made better... as with anything else, all in all Clickbank is a truly accessible electronic network that ought to be perfect for individuals first getting rolling in marketing and affiliate marketing.

Printed by Libri Plureos GmbH in Hamburg,
Germany